# Earth Day

## Rebecca Rissman

Heinemann Library
Chicago, Illinois

**www.heinemannraintree.com**
Visit our website to find out more information about Heinemann-Raintree books.

## To order:

☎ Phone 888-454-2279

 Visit www.heinemannraintree.com to browse our catalog and order online.

©2011 Heinemann Library
an imprint of Capstone Global Library, LLC
Chicago, Illinois

Edited by Adrian Vigliano and Rebecca Rissman
Designed by Ryan Frieson
Picture research by Tracy Cummins
Leveling by Nancy E. Harris
Originated by Capstone Global Library Ltd.
Printed in China by South China Printing Company Ltd.

15 14 13 12 11 10
10 9 8 7 6 5 4 3 2 1

Library of Congress Cataloging-in-Publication Data
Rissman, Rebecca.
  Earth day / Rebecca Rissman.
    p. cm.—(Holidays and festivals)
  Includes bibliographical references and index.
  ISBN 978-1-4329-4057-7 (hc)—ISBN 978-1-4329-4076-8 (pb) 1.
Earth Day—Juvenile literature. 2. Environmental protection—Juvenile
literature. I. Title.
  GE195.5.R55 2011
  394.262—dc22

2009052857

## Acknowledgments

The author and publishers are grateful to the following for permission to reproduce copyright material: Corbis ©Tim Pannel **p.5**; Corbis ©Guenter Rossenbach **p.11**; Corbis ©Vasiliki Paschali/epa **p.12**; Corbis ©Viviane Moos **p.13**; Corbis ©Yi Lu **p.14**; Corbis ©Guenter Rossenbach **p.23a**; Getty Images/Mark Mann **p.4**; Getty Images/Panoramic Images **p.7**; Getty Images/Jeff Foott **p.8**; Getty Images/Jupiter Images **p.15**; Getty Images/Charley Gallay **p.19**; Getty Images/Charley Gallay **p.23b**; istockphoto ©John Clines **p.22**; NASA/Goddard Space Flight Center **p.6**; Photolibrary/Sandro Di Carlo Darsa/PhotoAlto **p.17**; Shutterstock ©michael ledray **p.9**; Shutterstock ©Stéphane Bidouze **p.10**; Shutterstock ©jordache **p.16**; Shutterstock ©Morgan Lane Photography **p.18**; Shutterstock ©Stephen Aaron Rees **p.20**; Shutterstock ©Pedro Tavares **p.21**; Shutterstock ©Stéphane Bidouze **p.23c**.

Cover photograph of children carrying boxes of recycling reproduced with permission of Getty Images/image Source. Back cover photograph reproduced with permission of Shutterstock ©Pedro Tavares.

Every effort has been made to contact copyright holders of any material reproduced in this book. Any omissions will be rectified in subsequent printings if notice is given to the publisher.

# Contents

What Is a Holiday? . . . . . . . . . . .4

Planet Earth . . . . . . . . . . . . .6

Pollution . . . . . . . . . . . . . . . .8

Cleaning Up Pollution . . . . . . .14

Celebrating Earth Day . . . . . . .16

Earth Day Symbols . . . . . . . . .20

Calendar. . . . . . . . . . . . . . .22

Picture Glossary . . . . . . . . . . .23

Index . . . . . . . . . . . . . . . .24

# What Is a Holiday?

A holiday is a special day.
People celebrate holidays.

Earth Day is a holiday.
Earth Day is in April.

# Planet Earth

Earth is a planet.

We live on Earth.

# Pollution

People have polluted parts of Earth.
Harmful materials people have
made pollute Earth.

Some of Earth's air is polluted.

Some of Earth's water is polluted.

Some of Earth's land is polluted.

Pollution hurts animals and plants.

Pollution hurts people, too.

# Cleaning Up Pollution

People can clean up pollution.

People can help Earth.

# Celebrating Earth Day

On Earth Day people are thankful for Earth.

People pick up litter.

People plant trees.
People march in parades.

Earth Day reminds us to take care
of Earth.

# Earth Day Symbols

The recycle sign is a symbol of Earth Day. It reminds us to recycle.

Pictures of Earth are symbols of
Earth Day.

# Calendar

Earth Day is on April 22.

# Picture Glossary

**litter**  waste people have dropped on the ground

**parade**  group of people marching together to celebrate something

**pollution**  harmful materials made by people, such as litter, gases, or chemicals. Air, water, or land can be polluted.

# Index

air 9

land 11

litter 17, 23

parade 18, 23

planet 6

pollution 8, 12, 13, 14, 23

recycle 20

water 10

**Note to Parents and Teachers**

**Before reading**

Explain that every year on April 22, we celebrate Earth Day, a time to honor the planet on which we live. Ask the children what they like about Earth – trees, water, snow, seasons, etc. Ask them to share ways they can help take care of the Earth (recycle, turn off unused lights, don't litter). Make a "reminder" list of the ideas that can be posted in the classroom.

**After reading**

Go on a nature walk and explore plants and trees in their natural setting. Remember, you don't need to be in a rural setting to take a nature walk. Urban areas are filled with natural wonders. Help your students observe some often overlooked growth – the tops of trees, colorful grasses, or plants growing in sidewalk cracks. While outside, ask each child to document what they see in a descriptive way – a drawing, a story, or a poem.